Jump and Shout

THE CHEERLEADERS

TRACY NELSON MAURER

Rourke
Publishing LLC
Vero Beach, Florida 32964

Project Assistance courtesy of Jennifer Tell, Dance and Cheer Factory, Forest Lake, Minnesota.

The author also extends appreciation to Mike Maurer, Kendall and Lois Nelson, the Rourke team, Melissa Martyr-Wagner, Princeton University, and the University of Minnesota Alumni Association.

Photo Credits: Cover, Title, pgs 7, 20, 33, 34, 38, 40, 41, 44 ©PHOTOSPORT.COM
pgs 10, 16, 25 ©Paul Martinez/PHOTOSPORT.COM
pgs 12, 31, 43 ©Peter Schlitt/PHOTOSPORT.COM
pg 5 from the Library of Congress
pg 42 ©JBL Professional
pgs 15, 18, 28, 30, 32, 35 ©PIR

Editor: Frank Sloan

Cover and page design: Nicola Stratford

Notice: This book contains information that is true, complete, and accurate to the best of our knowledge. However, the author and Rourke Publishing LLC offer all recommendations and suggestions without any guarantees and disclaim all liability incurred in connection with the use of this information.

Safety first! Activities appearing or described in this publication may be dangerous. Always work with a trained coach and spotters when learning new cheerleading skills.

Library of Congress Cataloging-in-Publication Data

Maurer, Tracy, 1965-
  The cheerleaders / Tracy Nelson Maurer.
    p. cm. -- (Jump and shout)
  Summary: "Cheerleaders blend amazing athletic skills and spirited talent to perform breathtaking stunts. They work hard to boost school pride and win over judges at stiff competitions. Coaches expect teamwork, dedication, good grades, and healthy attitudes"--Provided by publisher.
  Includes index.
  ISBN 1-59515-498-1 (hardcover)
  1. Cheerleading--Juvenile literature. I. Title. II. Series.

LB3635.M25 2006
791.6'4--dc22

                              2005012702

Printed in the USA

cg/cg

Rourke Publishing
1-800-394-7055
www.rourkepublishing.com
sales@rourkepublishing.com
Post Office Box 3328, Vero Beach, FL 32964

TABLE OF CONTENTS

Chapter 1

WAY BACK WHEN

File those girly-girl, fluff-and-flounce ideas of cheerleading way back in the history department. They're old. They're also historically wrong.

Cheerleading began as a guy thing. In 1884, Princeton University football fan Thomas Peebles yelled, "Ray, Ray, Ray! Tiger, Tiger, Tiger! Sis, Sis, Sis! Boom, Boom, Boom! Aaaaah! Princeton, Princeton, Princeton!"

Five years later, Johnny "Jack" Campbell took the idea further at a bleak University of Minnesota football game against the rival team from Northwestern University of Illinois. He stood up and

In the early days cheerleading was dominated by men.

used a megaphone to encourage the crowd to yell the school's new cheer, "Rah, Rah, Rah! Ski-u-mah! Hoo-rah! Hoo-rah! Varsity! Varsity! Minn-e-so-tah!" It worked. The fans roared and the team won.

"Yell Marshall" Campbell kept cheering. By 1899, he and five buddies had fired up some serious school pride with regular cheers and fight songs. They started a trend. Other colleges created "spirit clubs," too.

Women weren't allowed to join these pep clubs. This shouldn't surprise you. Universities had only recently begun admitting female students then, and women weren't even allowed to vote for their government leaders until 1920. Fighting for the right to cheer seemed lame when women lacked so many other rights.

"Rah, Rah, Rah! Ski-u-mah! Hoo-rah! Varsity! Minn-e-so-tah!" More than a century later, one of the first successful American cheers is still used by the University of Minnesota—although nobody really knows what it means. One school myth said "ski-oo" was a Native American battle cry. Some say "U-mah" blended the letters from **U**niversity of **M**innesot**a**. More likely, it was supposed to rhyme with "Minnesota." Whatever works!

Hooray for Females

World War II drew men away from the farms, factories, and universities. Women took their places in the workforce. Females also took over the guys' jobs rooting for the home teams.

When the war ended, many social rules changed. Cheerleading became an acceptable activity for girls. With few other athletic team options, girls quickly took over cheerleading at schools everywhere in America. People began thinking it was just for girls. Worse yet for the girly-girl **stereotype**, classmates often elected their cheerleaders. This happened well into the 1950s. No tryouts. No judges. You know it: "Popularity Contest" all the way.

A "popular" girl cheerleader peps up a crowd at a 1950s school rally.

Back then, girls certainly couldn't wear trousers to classes (denim jeans were unthinkable). Cheerleaders couldn't wear skirts above the knees. They wore heavy sweaters and ordinary shoes, not cushioned athletic shoes. Girls would get mighty sweaty and sore trying to do stunts in outfits like that. So, they usually didn't.

Not surprisingly, the cutie-pie stereotype blossomed. It's still around even now. But cheerleading has changed a lot since then.

Working toward Equal

Since the 1970s, **feminists**, scholars, school administrators, coaches, parents, cheerleaders, and wanna-be cheerleaders have fought for and against cheerleading. The federal government's 1972 Title IX Education Amendment focused attention on equal access for both sexes, and that stirred things up even more. Over time, people have pondered many cheerleading issues.

✿ Is cheerleading a sport? Sport teams compete during a certain season and require athletic talent.

✿ Is cheerleading an extracurricular activity instead? After-school groups often meet all school year, sometimes performing or participating in many school functions. Maybe cheerleading blends "sport" and "activity" unlike other school groups?

✿ Does cheerleading tell girls that they're best suited for supporting roles? Or does cheerleading help develop leadership skills?

✿ Why don't all-boy squads cheer for all-girl teams?

✿ Do boys cheer because they can't make the A-team? Or could it be that boy cheerleaders have figured out that cheering is a fun way to meet a lot of girl cheerleaders? Is that sexist?

✿ If research shows that most cheerleaders carry B-grade averages, then are cheerleaders really airheads like some people think?

✿ If sports equals entertainment, then are cheerleaders any less important than the players, band members, announcers, camera crews, or other people who add to the show?

Questions, questions, questions. Here's the answer: There are no easy answers.

Shedding stereotypes takes time—and not just for female cheerleaders fighting the pink-'n-perky image. Male cheerleaders have made a huge comeback despite the undeserved sissy stereotype. Sissies? Hardly! Strength, balance, and stamina are musts for these guys. Look, maybe tossing a football is as tough as tossing a cheerleader, but the game doesn't end if the football isn't caught.

Times have changed—both male and female cheerleaders hold important roles in this physically demanding team sport.

A cheerleader's job is to excite the crowd.

Chapter 2

ATHLETES WITH ATTITUDE

Today's cheerleaders can be all shapes and sizes, but they can't be wimps. The complex cheer routines and performances demand physically fit athletes—male and female—with positive attitudes, outgoing personalities, and intense dedication.

The cheerleader's first job is to lead the crowd's cheers. It sounds simple and, sometimes, it even looks simple.

Try this: Stomp—clap, clap. Stomp—clap, clap. Stomp—clap, clap.

Keep going. Feel the rhythm? Now think about *exactly how* you're stomping and clapping. Are your feet apart or close together? Does your stomping knee pump up high? Are your hands cupped or flat? Are they under your chin? Elbows tucked in? Don't forget to smile, smile, smile! That's just for starters. You haven't added words (all memorized, of course), shaken a **pompon**, or tried any stunts.

All those high-energy cheers, also called routines, usually feature cheerleaders moving and yelling in **unison**. Cheerleaders memorize the words to routines. They memorize the proper body form for each **gesture**, from simple clasps to advanced jumps. They also memorize their places and steps for each routine. Often a squad starts the school year with ten or so standard cheers, and the coach adds more during the year to keep the crowd's attention.

Clap Vs. Clasp

Cheerleaders use two main gestures to make sound with their hands. The extra noise accents the words, beat, or rhythm in a cheer.

1. The *clap* uses flat, straight hands. The fingertips and palms touch each other. The sound is sharp and snappy.

2. The *clasp* brings cupped hands together with the thumbs overlapping in an "X." Fingertips of one hand wrap around the other hand. The sound is low and loud.

Think Physical

Beyond brainpower, what physical skills do cheerleaders need? The fast moves and jumps draw on lung and heart power like all **cardiovascular** exercise does. Cardiovascular endurance is very important.

How about those tricky moves where some team members hold or toss a few cheerleaders into the air? Stunts require control, strength, and balance. To gain these skills, pre-teen cheerleaders might do push-ups, sit-ups, pull-ups, and other exercises that use only the body's own weight for resistance. These **plyometric** exercises are good for older cheerleaders (and everyone else!), too. By age 16, weightlifting with dumbbells or medicine balls can build muscle power.

Gymnastic or tumbling moves like cartwheels, back handsprings, and the splits, focus on flexibility and coordination.

Cheerleading also uses fast-paced and precise **choreography** that often borrows heavily from ballet, hip-hop, and other dance forms. Again, coordination and a sense of rhythm improve a cheerleader's performance.

Today's cheerleaders blend athletic and gymnastic skills, grace, and a sense of rhythm with crisp gestures, loud voices, and smiling faces. All of this takes practice—and lots of it. Most teams practice for at least an hour, usually two or three times each week. They also work out or cross-train in gymnastics or dance, too. School cheerleaders do this week after week, game after game, in the blazing sun or drenching rain or freezing snow—win or lose.

Not quite so simple, huh?

Sharp Moves

Ever notice how cheerleaders use sharp, crisp movements? That's the point: to get you to notice them! Otherwise, they'd look like any other fan along the sidelines.

Good posture leads to good form.

Students encourage their team by clapping, yelling, and wearing school colors.

Chapter 3

THE "LEADER" IN CHEERLEADER

Watch a professional American ball game—football, basketball, or baseball—and you'll see grown men yelling, clapping, and happily doing "the wave." Anybody can cheer from the bleachers. Standing in front of hundreds or thousands of fans takes guts. Then getting those fans to *cheer with you* takes something even more special.

What makes cheerleaders leaders? Cheerleaders enjoy attention. They communicate through words and body movement in ways that excite other people to follow along and share their **enthusiasm**. Leaders boost pride when their team is winning. They show sportsmanship when their team loses. Many cheerleaders build on their leadership skills during their school years and use those abilities throughout their lives.

Cheerleaders might not change the course of history (although a few certainly have), but they might help change the course of a game. Researchers have discovered a link between **verbal encouragement** and increased performance. No wonder coaches often ask for the cheerleading squad to attend tough games.

Peppy Presidents

Dwight D. Eisenhower, Ronald Reagan, and George W. Bush were cheerleaders before they became leaders of a nation. Hmm. First pep rallies, then political rallies. Mere coincidence?

Unpopular News

Leadership isn't always **glamorous**. Sometimes it stinks. Cheerleaders get snubbed just because they're cheerleaders. Let's see. They're too pretty, too popular, too good, too stuck-up, too prissy, too precious, and just too much. Jealousy ruffles the pompons in every school.

Sorry, there's more.

New cheerleader friends demand extra time. Old non-cheerleader friends feel left out. Jocks can treat cheerleaders like second-rate athletes. Brainy kids might "forget" to include cheerleaders.

If that's not nasty enough, some teachers may expect the cheerleaders to behave perfectly all the time. Still other teachers lower their expectations of cheerleaders and treat them like they're dumb.

Wise cheerleaders defend themselves from the clueless stereotype by making the school honor roll. They also show respect for adults, mind their manners, and limit their PDAs (public displays of affection).

Most squads lay down tough rules, too. They won't put up with skipping practices, games, events, or classes. The standard school rules are in effect 24/7 for cheerleaders: no smoking, no alcohol, no drugs, no cheating, and no other major no-nos.

Cheerleaders do more than cheer. They lead by example. Thoughtful actions help convince people that cheerleaders are bright, outstanding students who demonstrate positive leadership skills. The role model job means playing it straight—without even *bending* the rules.

So Why Cheer?

Friendly, outgoing cheerleaders thrive on public attention. They love the spotlight and the crowds. Is that you? Cheerleading will put your positive attitude to good use.

Some signs that you might make a good cheerleader:

❀ You cheer wildly from the stands with or without a uniform.

❀ "Yes" and other positive words come easily to you.

❀ Your enthusiasm and energy spill over into everything you do.

❀ Workouts and physical fitness appeal to you.

❀ You're a dedicated team player.

❀ You love performing in front of a crowd.

❀ You're willing work hard to improve, over and over again.

The cheerleading experience teaches lessons that last well past school days. Achieving goals boosts self-confidence. Juggling studying and cheerleading develops time-management skills. You learn to handle disagreements and resolve conflicts. You get a jump-start on teamwork, the kind that you'll probably use someday in a career.

Cheerleaders lead by example.

Working at Teamwork

Even when you ooze positive attitude, cheerleading squads can run into negative territory. Conflicts happen. That's not always bad! People disagree in the real world, too. How you handle yourself can help find solutions that work for the team.

✿ Forget the silent treatment or stewing. Nobody reads minds.

✿ Talk directly to the person at the root of the problem and keep it between you two. Rallying support or tackling the issue in front of a group only stirs up more trouble.

✿ See the situation from the other person's view.

✿ Take responsibility for your part of the problem.

✿ Focus on facts, not how you feel. State what you see as the problem. Then listen carefully. Repeat back what you think you understood.

✿ Name-calling, threats, shouting, interrupting, blaming, and other rudeness make things worse.

✿ Ask for ideas to solve the problem. Look for a common goal and try to meet halfway.

✿ When you're stuck, ask for help. Find someone to hear both sides and offer a suggestion.

Chapter 4

TEAM PLAYERS

Cheerleading promotes teamwork. You learn to trust your team. You earn your team's trust in you. Every member plays an important part in the squad's success. This is true if you cheer for a school athletic team or if you cheer strictly for competitions, perhaps on a community all-star team.

Duty Descriptions

As a member of a team, you agree to pitch in. Every member takes on certain duties. Some of these duties stay the same for the entire year. For example, the coach and captain or co-captain roles usually don't change from game to game or contest to contest.

Who's Got Spirit?

Most cheerleading squads fall into one of two types. *School squads* cheer for student athletes. They may or may not enter cheerleading competitions. Cheerleaders on these teams usually include only students who attend that school.

All-star teams are not tied to school teams. Instead, they focus on competitions. Cheerleaders from across the community in different age levels can try out for all-star teams. A business, such as a for-profit studio, usually directs the all-star team, and members pay fees to join the squad.

However, the roles of Spotter, Base, and Flyer can change for each routine. Your coach might require you and your teammates to try all of these roles at least once, just so everyone understands all of the team duties.

COACH

(AKA Supervisor, General, Queen Mum)

Every team needs a coach, no matter what you call that person. Coaches set the rules and enforce them. They insist on safety. They attend training sessions to learn how to teach stunts. Coaches study technique, injury prevention, and the latest rules for schools or competitions. They arrange practices, exercises, and schedules. They help work on routines. They motivate each team member to achieve new goals and gain confidence. Coaches keep the team on track.

CAPTAIN OR CO-CAPTAIN

(AKA Your Royal Highness - just kidding!)

Although coaches make the final decisions, they may assign a leader or leaders from their squads to help give directions during the game or contest. Or, teams might elect their captains. The captain's duties could include calling which cheer to perform and starting the routine. Mostly, the captain should be a role model for the other team members. No tiaras, please.

BASE

(AKA Supporter, Lifter)

The base steadies the bottom of the stunt and supports the flyer. Bases are usually the stronger cheerleaders. They must hold their positions like statues. Staying still while balancing another person in the air takes concentration, too. A wobbly base can topple the stunt. The base also helps the flyer land, often with breathtaking catches.

FLYER

(AKA Mounter)

Snowboarders and skateboarders use **momentum** to catch big air. So does the flyer, but without a board, kneepads, or helmet. Talk about extreme! It's all about body power and teamwork. The flyer climbs, or mounts, the base, who helps hoist the flyer into an **aerial** position. The flyer's own momentum adds speed, grace, and height to the stunt. Flyers need tight balance and control, all the way up into the stunt and back down.

SPOTTER

(AKA Head Protectors)

Spotters, often the senior cheerleaders, trainers, or coaches, know every routine and watch for trouble. They stand ready to catch the flyer at any time, always on guard to keep the flyer's head from smacking the ground. Most team rules require spotters for performance stunts and learning new moves. Back spotters stand at the rear of the formation and catch the flyers. Back spotters should be strong, focused, and responsible.

MANAGER

(AKA the coach's Handy Helper)

Managers are often extremely dedicated cheerleading fans. Sometimes injured cheerleaders help manage the team. Next season's potential cheerleaders (people who didn't make the squad at tryouts this year) sometimes become managers. Alumni cheerleaders or parents also serve as managers. Managers make the coach's job less frantic. Their duties cover everything from booking buses to ordering uniforms. They handle paperwork, join pep rally committees, and fill water bottles.

PARENTS, FRIENDS, AND FAMILIES

(AKA the Cheerleaders' Cheerleaders)

Parents, families, and friends play a big part in a cheerleading team's success. Parents, especially, spend time driving their kids to practices and games and events. They donate money and time, even when they might not have much extra of either one. Thank them. Then thank them again and again!

Chapter 5

BEYOND POMPONS

Cheerleading isn't for everybody or every body. Not all schools offer cheerleading opportunities. Some schools don't even have sport teams to cheer for.

Don't despair. You still have options!

Many schools or community organizations support a variety of performance groups—from cheerleading squads to flag teams and from precision dancing to baton twirling organizations. These **pageantry arts** also include marching band and drum corps. Pageantry arts deliver powerful pizzazz in any shape, form, or venue!

Think of the performers who dazzle the crowds during the Olympics' opening and closing ceremonies. Or think of performers in local halftime shows, homecoming parades, and pep rallies. Like cheerleaders, these stars combine special skills and techniques with physical abilities to fire up a crowd.

A marching band and drill team take the field at halftime.

The Guards

Cheerleaders use their bodies and voices to express team support. Color guard and winter guard members use their bodies and flags for expression. The movements create visual harmony—flowing, twirling, and spinning to the music. Guard members usually perform in unison as cheerleaders do, and they love that big crowd reaction!

What's the Difference?

Color Guard	Winter Guard
Performs outdoors, often with a marching band in a wide open area or parade route	Performs indoors, often with pre-recorded music, props, and sets; one of the fastest growing pageantry arts
Features bright flag colors, usually school colors to promote school spirit	Features dramatic flag colors, usually to match the musical theme for a show or contest
Ribbons or streamers might replace flags for certain performances	Rifles, sabers, and other props might replace flags for certain performances
Costumes match the marching band or school colors	Costumes match musical theme

Wave Words

Guard members usually avoid the term "flag twirlers." The name isn't serious enough for their hundreds of hours of practice and rich military history (soldiers have defended their flags since the Egyptians). Some people call the guards the "silk lines," because flags were originally made of silk.

Military Influence

Color guard and winter guard grew directly from the military's flag carriers, called the honor guard. Since about 3000 B.C.E., soldiers have carried a national flag into battle and fiercely guarded it.

After World War II, American soldiers and members of the American Legion and Veterans of Foreign Wars started competing. They showed off fancy flag maneuvers and choreography set to solo drum rhythms. Music replaced the drum in the 1970s. Eventually the American flag was replaced with colorful fabrics to match the music, and the military influence gave way to dramatic routines.

Today's rifle twirling and baton twirling also spun off from military **maneuvers**. Precision dance and performance marching band took cues from the military, too.

Eastern European and Asian armies followed a rifle twirler as they marched. The **mace** eventually replaced the rifle. Some drum majors and majorettes still use a mace to lead marching bands.

The long, heavy, and off-balance mace didn't twirl very well. Then shorter, lighter, and more balanced batons came along. Men and women could twirl and toss—and, importantly, catch—the new batons. By the 1930s, female baton twirlers had joined the all-male marching bands.

(Opposite)
A color guard team performs center stage at a college bowl game.

(Right)
Uniforms and flag colors match school colors.

41

About the same time that baton twirling gained popularity, theatrical producers adopted the idea of dancers stepping in unison as soldiers did. The 1922 *Ziegfeld Follies* featured precision dancers. Three years later, Russell Markert translated the idea into the American troupe that eventually became the world-famous Radio City Music Hall Rockettes in New York City.

The Rockettes brought the military's passion for **uniformity** to center stage. Today's precision dance teams, also called drill teams, combine the artistry of color guards, ballet, tap, jazz, and modern dance. Their showmanship features the **accuracy** of twirlers and the enthusiasm of cheerleaders.

Rockette Size

The Radio City Rockettes company showcases 36 high-kicking dancers, all standing between 5'6" and 5'10-½" in height. Like the uniformity of the Rockettes, the precision footwork in *Riverdance* and the energetic drum-corps motif of Broadway's *Blast!* have captivated audiences everywhere, building even more momentum for the pageantry arts.

The Rockettes perform with military-style precision.

Suit Up, Mascots!

If you're a dancer or cheerleader, you usually work the crowds with your team. A **mascot**, however, is a solo cheerleader, dancer, and clown all stuffed into one hot costume. Even on a cold day, temperatures inside a mascot uniform with a head mask can reach 100°F (about 37°C).

These tigers, birds, and other mascot creatures have their own code of conduct. They never remove their heads in public (scary for kiddies and it ruins the effect). They usually never speak or yell. They use body gestures, or **pantomime**, to show their school spirit. It's not easy. Most mascots never reveal their true identity. They don't get any credit. But if you don't make the cheerleading squad, you might find that you're happy in that big fluffy suit!

Mascots dress in unique and colorful costumes with masks that hide their true identities.

43

Three Cheers for the Real World

Cheerleaders and pageantry artists master more than choreography and technique. They learn about traditions, commitment, honor, and attitude. How do they put that to work in the real world?

A few cheerleaders actually work as cheerleaders for professional teams, especially national football teams. They do all the work other college and high school cheerleaders do. They also get paid to attract fans to games by appearing on TV programs, in special shows, or in magazines. They pose for photos and sign autographs at games, at malls, in parades, and nearly anywhere else. They're always in the spotlight, even when they're not "working."

Serious cheerleaders also become business owners. They operate dance and cheer studios, run cheer camps, or open stores for uniform and gear, for example.

Cheerleaders take their enthusiasm, energy, and leadership skills into every type of career. It's an experience that lasts a lifetime.

Professional dance teams are often spotlighted on televised games.

Further Reading

Cheerleading in Action by John Crossingham. Crabtree Publishing Company, New York, New York, 2003.

Let's Go Team: Cheer, Dance, March / Color Guard Competition by Terry Usilton. Mason Crest Publishers, Philadelphia, 2003.

The Ultimate Guide to Cheerleading by Leslie Wilson. Three Rivers Press, New York, New York, 2003.

Web Sites

American Association of Cheerleading Coaches and Advisors
http://www.aacca.org/

CheerHome.com, an online information clearinghouse
http://www.CheerHome.com/

Drum Corps International
http://www.dci.org

National Cheerleaders Association
http://www.nationalspirit.com/

National Council for Spirit Safety & Education
http://www.spiritsafety.com/

United Performing Association, Inc.
http://www.upainc.net/

United States Twirling Association
http://www.ustwirling.com/

Universal Cheerleaders Association
http://www.varsity.com

Winter Guard International
http://www.wgi.org

World of Pageantry
http://worldofpageantry.com

Glossary

accuracy (AK yuh ruh see) — without mistake or error, correctness

aerial (AIR ee ul) — in the air or overhead

cardiovascular (KARD ee oh VAS kyoo lur) — the heart and blood, especially as they work with the lungs to supply oxygen to the body

choreography (KOR ee OG ruh fee) — the plan or patterns for dance steps, movement, or action, usually set to music

enthusiasm (en THOO zee AZ um) — excitement or lively interest

feminists (FEM uh nists) — people who believe women should have rights equal to men

gesture (JES chur) — hand or arm movement

glamorous (GLAM uh rus) — charming, dazzling, magical

mace (MAYS) — a tall, metal pole weighted at one end; often used by the leader of a marching band or soldiers

maneuvers (muh NYU vurz) — movements or actions

mascot (MAS KOT) — an animal, person, or thing used by a group as its symbol to bring good luck

momentum (moh MENT um) — force or speed of movement

pageantry arts (PAJ en tree ARTS) — the various types of performance groups, such as precision drill teams, color guard, or winter guard

pantomime (PANT uh MYM) — hand or arm movements that have meanings or show emotion

plyometric (PLY uh MEH trik) — in exercises, movements that use the body's own weight to build strength

pompon (POM pon) — in cheerleading, the tufted accessory used to add movement, color, and sound to performances; some dictionaries also use pompom or pom-pom

stereotype (STAIR ee oh TYP) — right or wrong, a commonly believed and simple image or idea about a group of people

uniformity (YOO nuh FOR mut ee) — sameness

unison (YOO nuh sun) — something done the same way at the same time

verbal encouragement (VUR bul en KUR ij munt) — sounds or words, such as cheers, spoken to help someone or something reach a goal

Index

About The Author

Tracy Nelson Maurer specializes in nonfiction and business writing. Her most recently published children's books include the *Roaring Rides* series, also from Rourke Publishing LLC. A former drum majorette and color guard member, Tracy lives near Minneapolis, Minnesota with her husband Mike and their two children.